science
technology
design

SCIENCE IN OUR WORLD

SCIENCE
and
DESIGN

Contributory Author
Brian Knapp, BSc, PhD
Art Director
Duncan McCrae, BSc
Special scientific models
Tim Fulford, MA, Head of Design and Technology,
Leighton Park School
Editorial consultants
Rita Owen, BSc and Sarah George, BEd
Special photography
Ian Gledhill
Illustrations
David Woodroffe
Science advisor
Jack Brettle, BSc, PhD,
Chief Research Scientist, Pilkington plc
Print consultants
Landmark Production Consultants Ltd
Printed and bound in Hong Kong
Produced by
EARTHSCAPE EDITIONS

First published in the United Kingdom in 1993
by Atlantic Europe Publishing Company Limited,
86 Peppard Road, Sonning Common, Reading,
Berkshire, RG4 9RP, UK
Telephone 0734 723751; Fax 0734 724488

Publication Data
Knapp, Brian
Science and design – (Science in our world; 23)
1. Science – For children
2. Design – For children
I. Title   II. Series
507
ISBN 1-869860-92-6

In this book you will find some words that have been shown in **bold** type. There is a full explanation of each of these words on pages 46 and 47.

Experiments that you might like to try for yourself have been put in a yellow box like this.

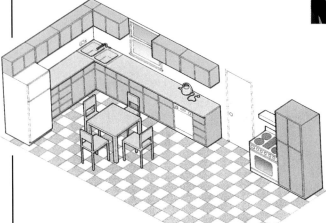

Acknowledgements
The publishers would like to thank the following:
Bausch & Lomb U.K. Ltd, Janet Brettle, Leighton Park
School, Marcia Young, Pelvic Posture Ltd and Redlands
County Primary School.

Picture credits
t=top b=bottom l=left r=right
All photographs are from the Earthscape Editions library.

Contents

Introduction

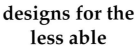

Are you sitting comfortably? If so this is probably because someone has spent much time and effort shaping – designing – the chair so that it fits you well.

Designs must work well, but they are best when they are easy and safe – appropriate – for people to use. To discover what is an appropriate design it is important to understand how people vary in size and shape. Because we use our bodies to lift, pull or push things it is also necessary to understand the **forces** that act on our bodies. For example, we often use our arms much like a crane. When we lift a pan or a bag the arm bones do the same job as the long boom of a crane, with the **pivot**, called a joint, at one end. Good designs will minimise the forces that could tear at our

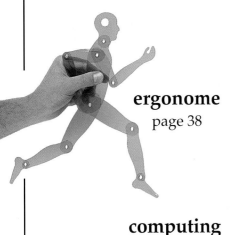
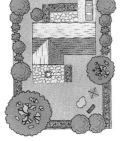

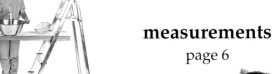

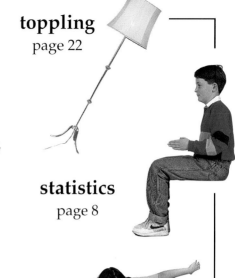

muscles and instead they will use our muscles to best advantage.

Understanding the scientific principles of size, shape and **behaviour** make it much easier to design an item that is suitable for its purpose, whether it may be the complicated interior of a spacecraft, a school chair, fashion clothes and even an apparently simple thing such as a toothbrush.

Without a good basis for design large amounts of effort can be wasted because things are much less likely to be easy and convenient to use. Continued use of things with a poor design can also lead to health and safety problems.

Find out about the world of design, safety and convenience in any way you choose. Just turn to any page to make your discoveries.

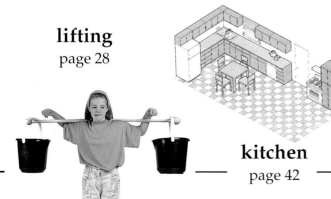

Are we all the same?

Before we try to design an object for use, we have to understand about the variety in people. This is because, although people have many features in common, they vary enormously in detail. Any design must therefore cater for as many sizes and shapes as possible.

Height and **weight** are obvious ways that people differ. But their body shapes differ in many other ways as well. If you measure many people you soon find out how varied they are and how far a single design needs to cater for many different sizes and shapes.

Big mouth?
Many snacks are designed to be popped into the mouth whole. How would you measure a number of people to see how big their mouths are? Ask some volunteers to have their wide-open mouths measured for height and width using a ruler. Record the results.

Now try again, using pieces of bread cut into cubes and 'fingers'. For each person record the size of the biggest piece of each shape they can get into their mouths and still chew easily. Is there as big a variety as in mouth sizes? From your results can you suggest why many snack bars are the size and shape they are?

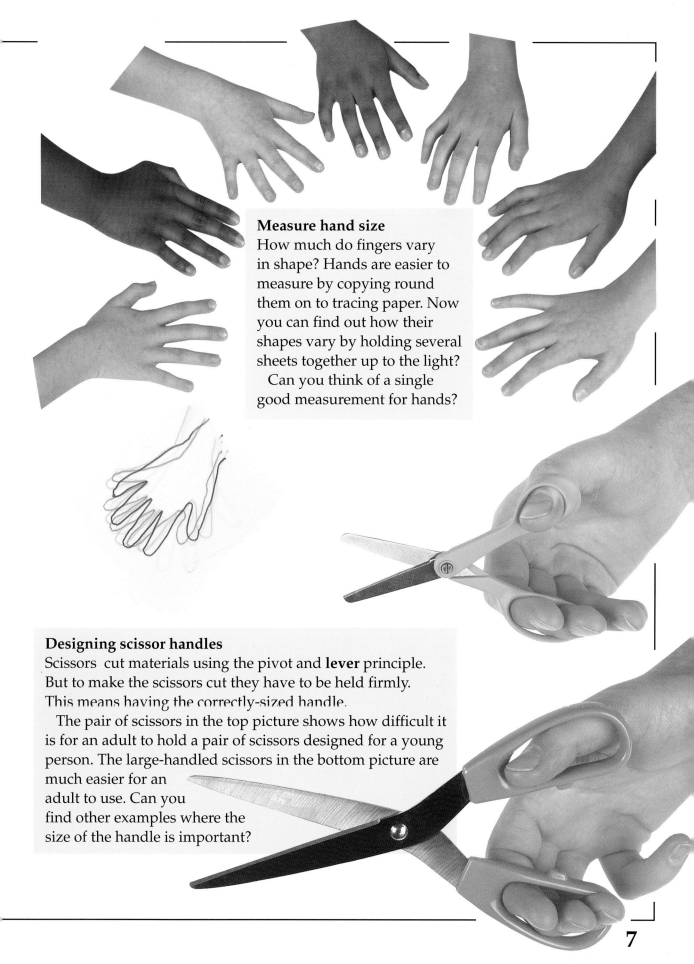

Measure hand size

How much do fingers vary in shape? Hands are easier to measure by copying round them on to tracing paper. Now you can find out how their shapes vary by holding several sheets together up to the light?

Can you think of a single good measurement for hands?

Designing scissor handles

Scissors cut materials using the pivot and **lever** principle. But to make the scissors cut they have to be held firmly. This means having the correctly-sized handle.

The pair of scissors in the top picture shows how difficult it is for an adult to hold a pair of scissors designed for a young person. The large-handled scissors in the bottom picture are much easier for an adult to use. Can you find other examples where the size of the handle is important?

7

Vital statistics

Some typical measurements made of seated people.

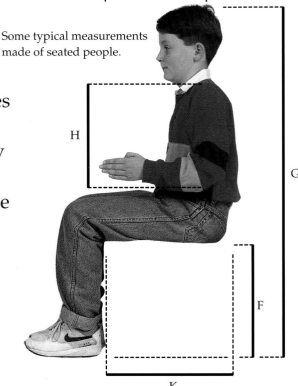

As you get older your body changes its dimensions. People get taller because their bones grow until they are in their mid teens. For the next 30 years or so they remain about the same height (although they may become fatter), but as they become elderly the spine **compresses** and people get slightly shorter.

These changes have to be considered when designing things to be used. This is why it is so important to measure the sizes and shapes of people.

F is the height of the top of a hard seat when the sitter has their upper leg horizontal and the lower leg vertical.

Measuring seated height. A chair with height adjustment (see page 16) would be the easiest to use (see page 38). However, upturned buckets can be stacked to give an approximate horizontal seating height.

Measurements in metres	9-year-olds		13-year-olds		Adults		Elderly people	
	Girls	*Boys*	*Girls*	*Boys*	*Women*	*Men*	*Women*	*Men*
Standing overhead reach (A)	1.65	1.65	1.90	1.90	2.10	2.2	1.90	2.0
Height to the top of the head (B)	1.40	1.40	1.55	1.55	1.60	1.70	1.50	1.65
Standing eye level (C)	1.20	1.20	1.40	1.40	1.50	1.60	1.40	1.55
Shoulder to fingertip length (D)	0.60	0.60	0.70	0.70	0.70	0.80	0.65	0.75
Hip height (E)	0.70	0.70	0.80	0.85	0.80	0.90	0.75	0.85
Height of bottom when seated (F)	0.35	0.35	0.40	0.40	0.40	0.45	0.40	0.40
Head height when seated (G)	0.70	0.70	0.80	0.80	0.85	0.90	0.80	0.85
Shoulder-elbow length (H)	0.20	0.20	0.25	0.25	0.30	0.37	0.31	0.35
Elbow-fingertip length (J)	0.35	0.35	0.40	0.40	0.45	0.50	0.40	0.45
Upper leg length (K)	0.40	0.40	0.45	0.45	0.50	0.50	0.45	0.45

Sizes are for 'European' people

How does your class compare?

For each person in your class, measure some of the distances shown on these pictures. Now find the average for each distance by adding up all the measurements and dividing by the number of people measured. This is easy to do with a calculator.

For example, if there are 10 people in your class and you measure their heights as 1.40, 1.45, 1.49, 1.55, 1.53, 1.54, 1.50, 1.58, 1.38, 1.50, then adding all the heights gives 14.92 m. To get the average divide by 10 (the number in the class), to give the answer 1.49.

What happens if you separate boys from girls and work out the average heights for both groups? Does this match the answers given in the table on the opposite page?

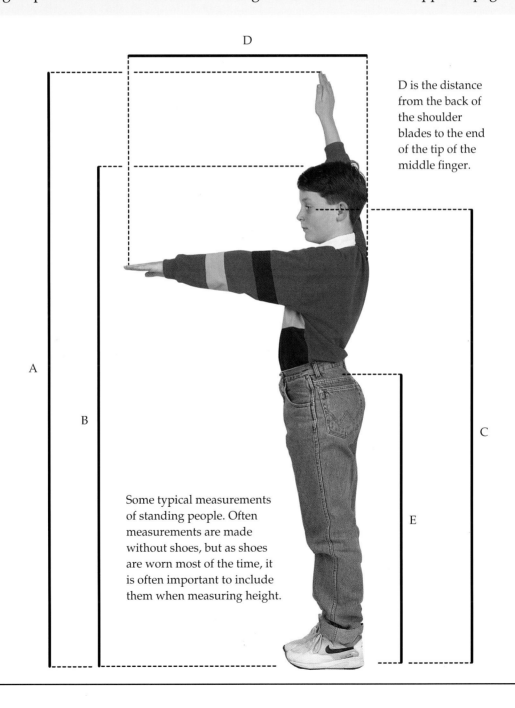

D

D is the distance from the back of the shoulder blades to the end of the tip of the middle finger.

A

B

C

E

Some typical measurements of standing people. Often measurements are made without shoes, but as shoes are worn most of the time, it is often important to include them when measuring height.

Making use of measurements

How do people find out what is a suitable shape and size for a design? They can make it to match their personal needs, they can take measurements of lots of people (as on page 9) and make the design fit the middle-sized, or **average**, person, or they can try to make the design suitable for as many people as possible. Measurements give information that can be used for decision making.

If all chairs were made to fit younger children then this is how adults might look when sitting down!

If all clothing were made to fit the average adult then this is how you might look when attending school!

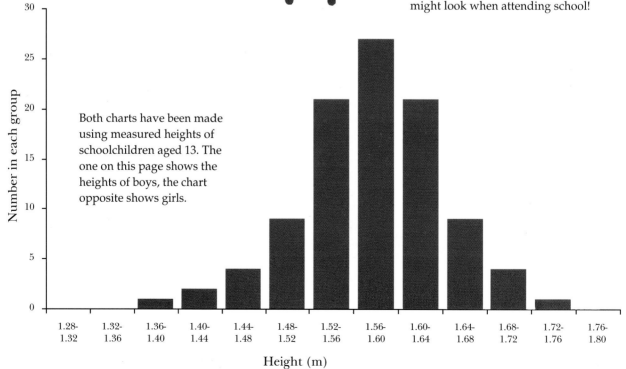

Both charts have been made using measured heights of schoolchildren aged 13. The one on this page shows the heights of boys, the chart opposite shows girls.

Number in each group

Height (m)

Check common beliefs

See if you can find answers to check whether the following statements are true:

1. This design is suited to me and therefore it will suit everyone.
2. This design is made for the average person and therefore it will suit everyone.
3. People vary so much in size that they can't all be catered for, but as people are so adaptable it doesn't matter anyway.

Charts that measure ranges of size

The measurements you have made will show you that we vary in size. So how do we use this knowledge to help us in design? It is often very difficult to make sense of numbers written out as tables, so it is often easier to understand what is happening by making a chart of the results. There are three steps to making a chart (in this case for height):

1. Measure a group of people (at least 20).
2. Make a column chart like the one shown below.
3. You can see that most people fit into just a few columns and that more people fit in to one column than any other.

These charts help people to decide whether to design for everyone, most people, or the most common group of people.

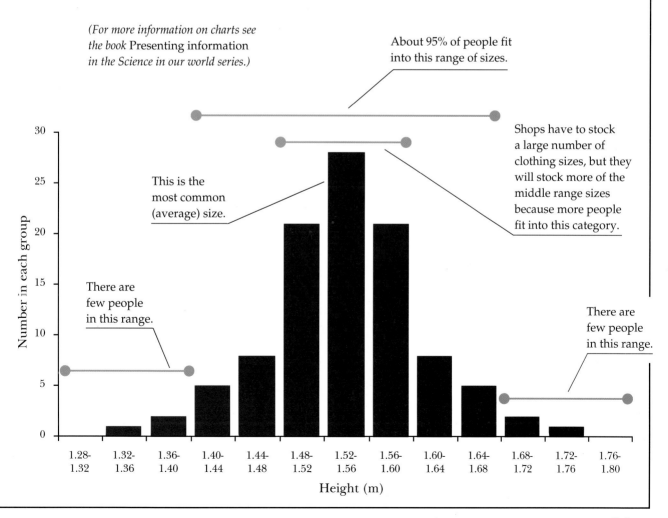

(For more information on charts see the book Presenting information *in the Science in our world series.)*

About 95% of people fit into this range of sizes.

Shops have to stock a large number of clothing sizes, but they will stock more of the middle range sizes because more people fit into this category.

This is the most common (average) size.

There are few people in this range.

There are few people in this range.

Number in each group

Height (m)

Can one size fit all?

A toothbrush is a very common tool, with an extremely important job. But when you go into a shop there are very few sizes of toothbrush to choose from, usually 'childrens' and 'adults'. Perhaps one brush will have a slightly smaller head than another, but the sizes and shapes within each group will not vary widely in the way that, for example, clothes might come in a wide range of sizes and fittings. This is because the design of a toothbrush has cleverly evolved to meet a 'one toothbrush fits all' principle. This is why.

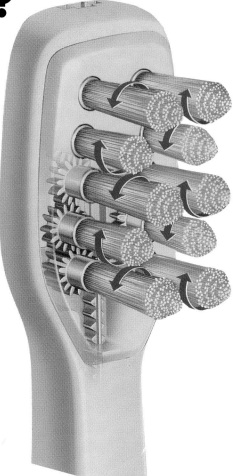

Life without toothbrushes
If you do not have a toothbrush, you have to find some other tool to clean your teeth. One way is to use your finger as a brush. You will soon find that the smooth surface of a finger and its rounded shape is a poor brush.

The head of this electric toothbrush is made so that each of the tufts can spin. This action cleans the teeth without the brush having to be moved up and down. Notice how the brush head is still the usual shape so that the tufts can reach the smallest crevices between teeth.

Why one size works
One size fits all because the brushes are designed to be scrubbed across the teeth. The brushing action ensures that all the teeth are cleaned whether they are large or small. The design has to match the smallest crevices that must be reached. As a result, there is no need for widely varying brush sizes.

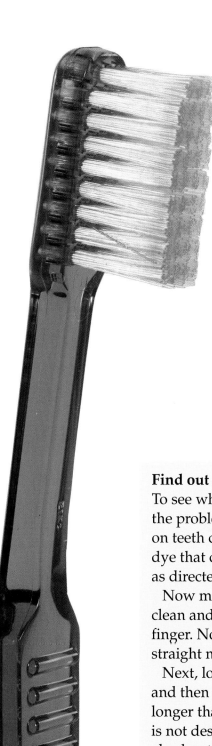

Straight or curved?

A toothbrush head is usually straight, not curved like your mouth. If it were curved do you think this would make it easier or harder to use ?

Find a straight and a curved scrubbing brush and try each in turn on a number of curved household objects such as pots and pans. Which can be used in more situations?

Repeat this experiment with long and short scrubbing brushes. Which can be used in more places? Does this explain why toothbrushes have much the same shape?

Find out about brushing

To see what design is needed, you must know the problem to be solved. The remains of food on teeth can be shown by using a special dental dye that can be bought from a pharmacy. Use it as directed then look at the pattern of colour.

Now make sure your hands are completely clean and try rubbing the dye away with a finger. Notice that your finger is mostly held straight no matter which tooth you are rubbing.

Next, look carefully at the head of a toothbrush and then compare it with your teeth. The head is longer than any of your teeth because the brush is not designed to clean your teeth one by one. It also has to clean 'round' and in between your teeth as well as cleaning your gums.

(For more information on teeth and the effect of the special colouring agent see the book Food *in the Science in our world series.)*

Find the right height

It is important to make our environment as convenient to work in as possible. This means making working surfaces, for example, at heights that will allow our muscles to work as efficiently as possible and not become tired.

In general your arms work best when the elbow is at right angles and when the back is straight.

Kitchens are common places where many different jobs have to be done. It is particularly important that the correct working height is achieved.

The ladder and board arrangement shown here will allow you to investigate how easy it is to work at a number of different heights. An adjustable ironing board will also give you a range of heights to experiment with.

Cooking: surface should be 100 mm below elbow height.

14

Eating: surface should be 50 mm above elbow height, so this table is too low.

Finding the right height

Try these activities while standing by a table made up of a board placed between two ladders: writing, vigorously stirring a liquid in a saucepan, rolling dough, eating from a bowl.

Is each activity comfortable if the board is kept at the same height?

Change the board height by placing it between different rungs of the ladders. Record the height at which the board was most comfortable for each activity.

Repeat the experiment for the same activities, but this time sit on a chair.

Craft work: surface should be level with elbow height.

Find out where differences are important

The statistics on page 8 might suggest the height of a working surface for different age groups. Ask some adults to do the tasks listed above. Can they work with the board at the same height as you can? Are there some tasks where the height is more important than others? What does this mean for the number of sizes of table that have to be made?

Are you computing comfortably?

Many people enjoy using a computer. It is easy to sit for hours in front of a computer monitor as you get carried away by the excitement of what you are doing.

But sitting for long periods can be bad for you, especially if you are sitting in the wrong position. Here are some of the measurements that help to provide healthy computing. How do you measure up?

1 Your eyes at rest look down at about 15 degrees from the horizontal. The centre of your monitor should be 15 degrees below your level line of sight and be tilted so that the whole screen is square on to you. The top of the screen will then be at eye level and the bottom of the screen at about 30 degrees from the horizontal.

This picture shows the way it is common for young people to sit while they are computing. The numbered captions explain the most healthy positions and suggest what this person would need to do to correct his sitting position.

2 The distance between your eyes and the screen should be 0.5 – 0.7 m to avoid eye strain.

3 The keyboard must be just below the height of your elbow. Slightly raise the height of the chair.

4 Your upper leg must be nearly horizontal. A footrest would correct this problem.

5 Your lower leg must be vertical. A footrest would correct this problem.

Correct posture

Correct posture means a comfortable and healthy sitting position. Look at each of the pictures on this page. Are either of the people sitting with the correct posture? Suggest what changes should be made in each case.

The right school and home computing chair

On page 8 you will find the dimensions of people of different ages. Suggest why it would be best to have chairs with adjustable heights in school classrooms where computers are in use.

Test your position

With the help of a friend, make a note of your sitting position while computing and compare them with the body-friendly positions given on the page opposite.

Were you sitting properly? If not, alter the seat, the computer screen and keyboard until you meet the body-friendly measurements. Now you know which is the most healthy way to sit, do you think the new position is also more comfortable? Do you think, in general, that computers, chairs and desks are designed primarily for adult use?

Testing your reach

Much of what we do depends on how far we can reach. For example, school desks should be designed to give enough space for you to perform the tasks you are asked to do, but if they are too big then parts of the desk will be wasted because they will be beyond your **reach**.

Vertical and horizontal reach

The picture above shows a person standing at a kitchen work-top. The horizontal reach while cooking is far less than that shown in the picture of a school table below. Stand at a kitchen work-top and try to find out why kitchen work-tops are narrow.

Find out your reach

Cover your desk with one large sheet or several small sheets of paper. Hold a pencil in your hand and, sitting naturally, draw a line to show the furthest distance you can reach.

If you can reach beyond the edges of the desk, go to a larger table and repeat the test.

Can you think why tables and desks are often rectangular when the shape of your reach is a curve?

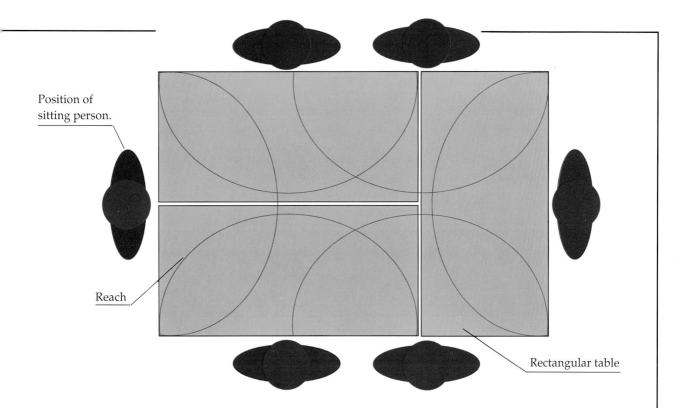

Position of sitting person.

Reach

Rectangular table

Group work

Much of what you do in class may be group work and for this several desks or tables may be put together. Use the technique shown opposite to find out if the desks work well when grouped together or is there wasted space or overcrowding?

Try to rearrange the desks to make the most use of them. Does this depend on the task you want to do? Would a different shape of desk help to remove the problem?

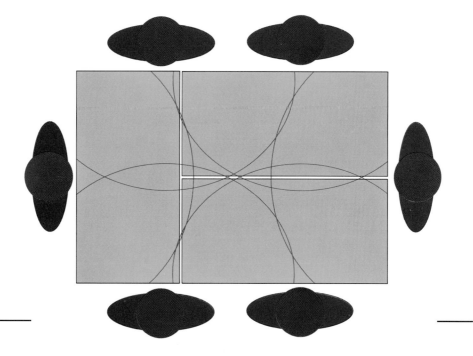

Understanding forces

If you stood a pencil on end you would not be surprised at how easy it was to knock over. Many objects are balanced very delicately, and although we may not always notice this, the results can be very important.

The key to stability is the **centre of gravity**. The centre of gravity of an object is the point at which it balances. All objects have a centre of gravity. However, because people can change their positions, their centre of gravity changes accordingly.

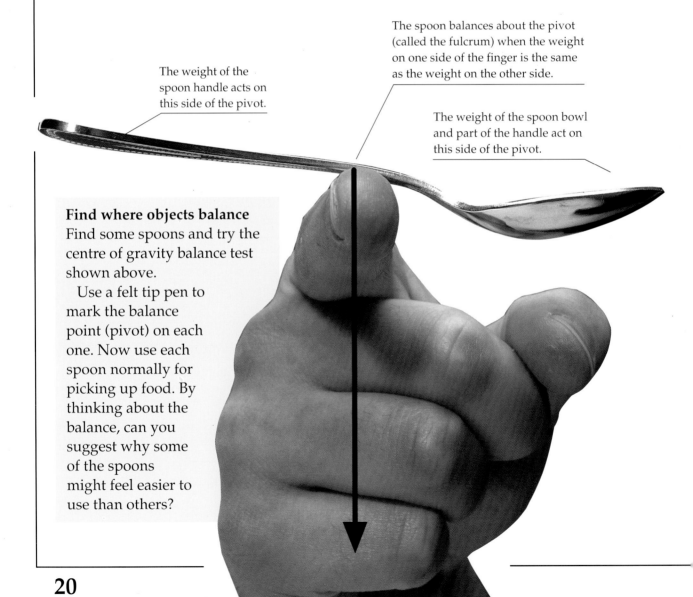

The spoon balances about the pivot (called the fulcrum) when the weight on one side of the finger is the same as the weight on the other side.

The weight of the spoon handle acts on this side of the pivot.

The weight of the spoon bowl and part of the handle act on this side of the pivot.

Find where objects balance
Find some spoons and try the centre of gravity balance test shown above.

Use a felt tip pen to mark the balance point (pivot) on each one. Now use each spoon normally for picking up food. By thinking about the balance, can you suggest why some of the spoons might feel easier to use than others?

The diagram above shows two sets of weights balanced on a board. It is used here and on other pages to help you to understand how complicated shapes can be thought of in terms of simple balancing forces.

On some pages a small weight is balanced by a large weight. This also shows the principle of levers.

(For more information on centres of gravity see the book Falling (Gravity) *and* Measuring *in the Science in our world series.)*

Centre of gravity

Each weight has its own centre of gravity. When the weights are equal and they are equal distances from the pivot, then the board will remain level.

When people hold something heavy such as a dumb-bell, they automatically adjust their posture (the way they stand) to put the centre of gravity over the legs. Notice how this girl has leaned back to balance the weights in her hands.

Centre of gravity (where the weight of the body acts).

21

Preventing toppling

Many things we use are pleasant to look at, but sometimes good looks may not make them easy to use.

For example, it is particularly important that fragile objects like standard lamps and containers for liquid should be stable and not topple over easily. To make sure this does not happen, designs have to incorporate a low centre of gravity.

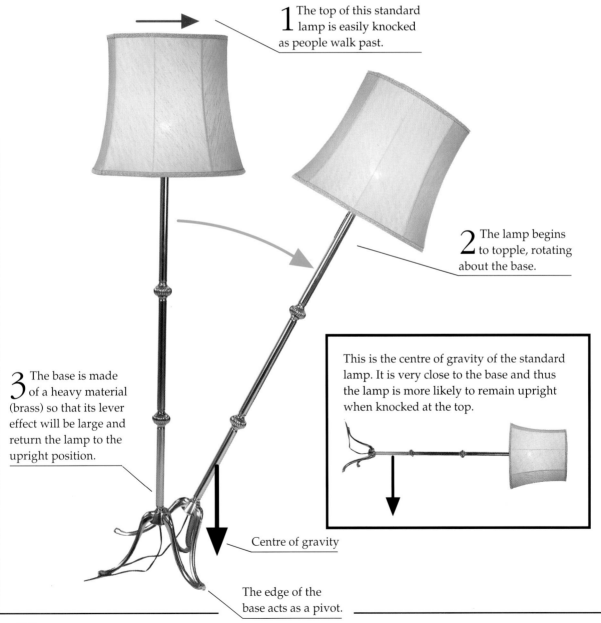

1 The top of this standard lamp is easily knocked as people walk past.

2 The lamp begins to topple, rotating about the base.

3 The base is made of a heavy material (brass) so that its lever effect will be large and return the lamp to the upright position.

This is the centre of gravity of the standard lamp. It is very close to the base and thus the lamp is more likely to remain upright when knocked at the top.

Centre of gravity

The edge of the base acts as a pivot.

Stable containers

Containers are sometimes placed on sloping surfaces such as a grassy bank while out on a picnic. Therefore it is important to have picnic ware that will be as stable as possible.

To test some containers for yourself, get three different sized transparent containers and place the same volume of liquid in each one. Then place them one at a time on a board and lift one end slowly until the container tips over. Measure the angle that the board has been raised with a protractor.

Does the container with the highest level of liquid tip over first? How would this knowledge help you to design, for example, better table cups or better picnic ware?

(For more information on finding centres of gravity see the book Measuring *in the Science in our world series.)*

Board

Block can be moved to change the angle of the board.

Lip to stop container from sliding.

Keeping your balance

As you stretch out your arms you alter the balance of your body. The further you reach, the more the balance point moves away from over your legs and the more you are likely to topple over. Finding out how to prevent yourself from toppling over, in other words how to be stable, is important so that people can design environments which are safe to live and work in.

Both the weight (**mass**) of the object and the distance from the pivot have important influences on balance. This is why a small object a long way from the pivot can balance a large one, or why your body can become unbalanced by a small object held at arms length.

Stretching out: the effect of the dumb-bell causes the pivot point to move out in front of your body.

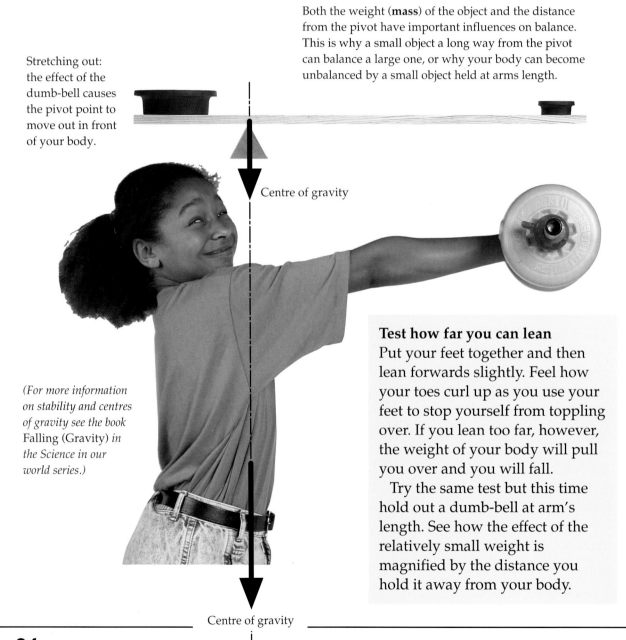

Centre of gravity

(For more information on stability and centres of gravity see the book Falling (Gravity) in the Science in our world series.)

Test how far you can lean
Put your feet together and then lean forwards slightly. Feel how your toes curl up as you use your feet to stop yourself from toppling over. If you lean too far, however, the weight of your body will pull you over and you will fall.

Try the same test but this time hold out a dumb-bell at arm's length. See how the effect of the relatively small weight is magnified by the distance you hold it away from your body.

Centre of gravity

Very young children do not have a good sense of balance. It is important, therefore, that the guard rail is taller than the complete body height of young children.

Guard rails prevent toppling action. If you leans too far, the top of a guard rail becomes the pivot. Because your lower trunk is heavier than your upper trunk it is difficult to overbalance with a pivot at your stomach.

If you reach too far you are likely to topple forwards because your centre of gravity will be in front of your foot.

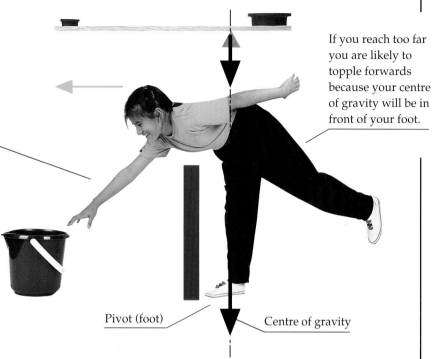

Pivot (foot) Centre of gravity

Safety rail

When you reach out a long way the centre of gravity moves away from the body and you begin to topple (see page 22).

Guard rails, whether they are on exposed stairways of buildings, or next to machines, are designed to make it difficult for people to topple into danger.

A guard rail will stop the inner leg from toppling and provide a support.

Find out about guard rail height

Guard rails seem to be made in many heights. Test how the height changes by using the ladders and board (see page 14). Try leaning across the board at various heights while holding a heavy bag.

Can you find the lowest height for safety?

Guard rails are found in all public places, such as this shopping centre in Toronto, Canada. The rail only has to be high enough to prevent toppling. This is why guard rails do not have to be, for example, two metres high.

Making use of levers

Most of the actions we make involve pulling, pushing or turning. These are all forces. So when people design things that are to be used they need to make sure that our arms, legs and body – the natural levers of our bodies – will work efficiently.

An adult holding a stack of books with one hand.

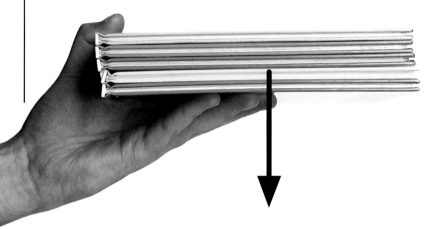

Ease of use

If you ask both an adult and an 7-year-old each to hold a stack of books balanced on their hand as shown in these pictures, you will find that the 7-year-old has much greater difficulty because more of the stack hangs over the end of their hand.

Because the balancing point of the stack is beyond their hand, the thumb has to work harder to hold the stack level. The same problem would arise if you were carrying a plateful of food across, say, a cafeteria where there were lots of people about and it was important to be able to walk around and hold the food steady. Clearly smaller plates, trays and other carrying objects are easier than large ones for younger people to carry.

A 7-year-old with the same stack of books. Notice how the fingers do not reach as far as the balancing point.

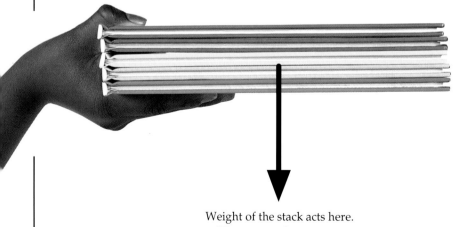

Weight of the stack acts here. (The centre of gravity, or balancing point.)

Turning angle

Try turning a variety of knobs (such as a door knob and a tuning knob on a radio) and twist them from side to side as far as you are able to without changing your grip. Make a mark against the farthest you can turn in each direction. Is your turning angle equal in each direction (known as **symmetrical**)?

While turning each knob feel how hard you have to grip the knob to stop it slipping. Are big knobs easier to handle than small ones?

Try finding out why your control of a bicycle is better when you hold the ends of the handlebars rather than near the central post.

Cranes are designed on the principle of pivots and levers. See how many levers and pivots you can find in this example.

Leverage increases this way.

The nut is the pivot.

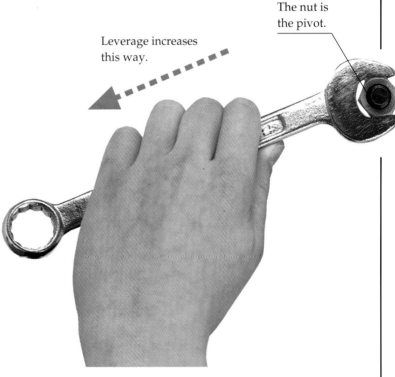

A spanner is used to apply leverage to a nut. However, people are not always aware of the amount of force they need to apply to the spanner, so the designer has to ensure that the spanner is not so long that users can over-tighten the nut and strip the thread.

Lifting with ease

We need to be very careful how we use our bodies because, although they are tough, they can be damaged. So it makes sense to think about the problems that have to be faced and the ways of coping with them. One common area that causes problems is muscle strain through lifting heavy objects the wrong way. Here you can see how to make lifting easier, and why some designs for carrying heavy objects are better than others.

Removing the strain
There are many things that have to be lifted and carried. For example, when shopping people have heavy bags to carry.

Carrying one shopping bag means that there is a heavy weight one side of the body with nothing to **counterbalance** it on the other side. Carrying one bag can damage the spine; so a simple remedy is to share the load between two bags, although using a trolley would be much better.

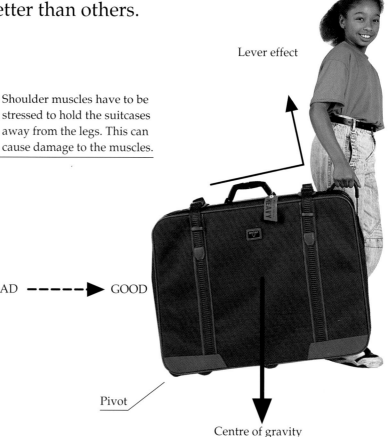

Lever effect

Shoulder muscles have to be stressed to hold the suitcases away from the legs. This can cause damage to the muscles.

BAD - - - - -> GOOD

Suitcases move inwards

Centre of gravity

Pivot

Centre of gravity

A person carrying heavy suitcases puts enormous stress on the bones and muscles near their spine. This can lead to backache and even injury.

It is far more comfortable to let the weight be carried by small wheels built in to the case. Heavier weights can be carried without any risk of injury to the carrier.

These market sellers in Thailand use a carrying pole with built-in springiness. The weight is carried on their shoulder. It would be impossible to carry such weights in bags held by the side.

Carrying poles

Make up a traditional carrying pole (called a yoke) and walk about to see how it feels. First try the pole on one shoulder and then try it placed across the back of the neck. Which is best for balance?

Find out about balancing forces

Pick up a bag and put some books in it, just enough to be heavy and pull you to one side. Now look in a full-length mirror at the way you are standing.

The weight of the bag will have made your spine curve in a sideways arc and you will have raised your free arm as your body automatically tries to produce a counterbalance.

Next transfer half of the books to another bag and hold this in the other hand to provide a counterbalance. Now the spine should be straight. But to walk you must hold the bags out or they will bump against your sides. Try walking around until you can sense which parts of your body are beginning to feel tired.

Compare the traditional way of carrying heavy weights with the modern way of carrying bags.

Centre of gravity

Design for safety

Understanding the way people behave is essential for making safe designs. Many accidents are caused when things are knocked over, for example. It may be a saucepan filled with scalding-hot water or an iron that falls over and burns a shirt on an ironing board. Many of these accidents can be prevented by designing things with safety in mind.

Plus and minus of design
Many items can be designed to make good use of the principle of forces, yet the very same properties can easily cause accidents. The saucepan shows this well. It is designed on the lever and pivot principle.

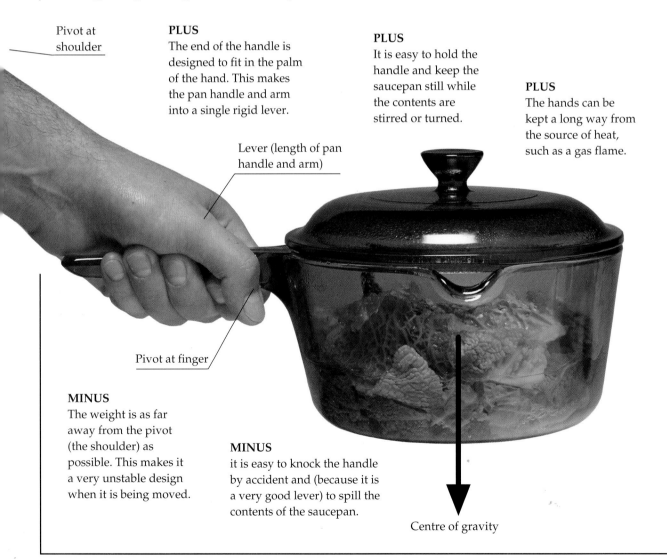

Pivot at shoulder

PLUS
The end of the handle is designed to fit in the palm of the hand. This makes the pan handle and arm into a single rigid lever.

PLUS
It is easy to hold the handle and keep the saucepan still while the contents are stirred or turned.

PLUS
The hands can be kept a long way from the source of heat, such as a gas flame.

Lever (length of pan handle and arm)

Pivot at finger

MINUS
The weight is as far away from the pivot (the shoulder) as possible. This makes it a very unstable design when it is being moved.

MINUS
it is easy to knock the handle by accident and (because it is a very good lever) to spill the contents of the saucepan.

Centre of gravity

Open fires need a guard to prevent people or objects touching parts that could burn or cause fires.

Designing away the problems

Once the minus features have been identified it is easier to design them away. The minus points on the saucepan shown on the opposite page can largely be overcome by adding a small carrying handle on the opposite side of the pan. Using two hands makes the pan more balanced during transport. The fire-guard and the mains lead shown in the pictures above are further common examples of safe design.

It is easy to trip over a mains lead lying on a floor. Leads that are coiled, such as the example shown here, reduce the risk of accidents.

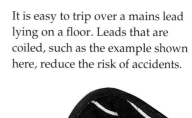

Is there a safe and easy design?

This pan is so heavy when it is full that it could not be lifted with a single handle. As a result there are no easy 'levers' to knock. So why isn't it used more often?

Place a number of items on a cooker including those with and without long lever handles and make a list of the plus and minus points to find out why large two handled pans are not used very often.

Easier opening

Opening and closing doors and lids is a very common activity. But some doors and lids are more difficult to operate than others. Here are some ways to design doors and lids so that the force needed to open them is as small as possible.

The lever and pivot
A door on a hinge is like a lever and pivot. The door is a lever and the pivot is the hinge.

The experiment below shows you that the farther you are away from the pivot, the less force is needed to operate it.

Opening force
To find the way that the opening force varies, make up a door like the one shown here, using a small hinge and a plank of wood with a door handle or cup hooks screwed into its surface. Alternatively, temporarily attach a row of rubber suckers to a normal room door.

Attach a spring balance to each hook or rubber sucker in turn and note the force needed to open the door.

Now plot a chart of force against distance of from hinge. What does this tell you about where to put the handle to open doors?

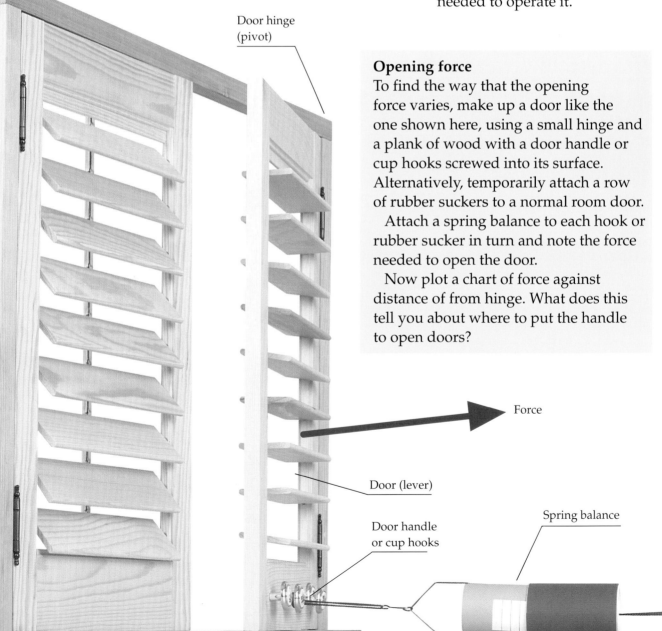

Door hinge (pivot)

Force

Door (lever)

Door handle or cup hooks

Spring balance

Placing the handles

Door handles and knobs are often placed for design reasons. But the closer the handle or knob is placed to the hinge the harder the door will be to open.

In the picture on the left four door knobs have been fitted to the cupboard door. The left hand knob is the one to use for opening the door most easily. Look around your school and home to find out if all handles and knobs are placed in the best positions for easy opening.

Improving the design

On the back of the cupboard door shown on the right there is a mechanism for adjusting the slats (called louvres). Look carefully at the mechanism and try to think of an easier way of moving the louvres, perhaps by making some kind of lever.

Designing for the less able

There are more elderly people in the world today than ever before. There are also people who have some kind of physical disability. But most of the things around the home are designed for active adults.
How can we use science and design to help everyone?

This tap has a smooth finish and is hard to turn for people with a weak grip.

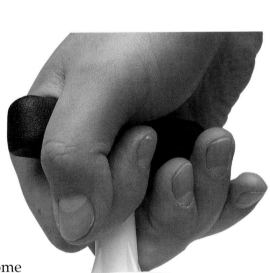

Leverage improves this way

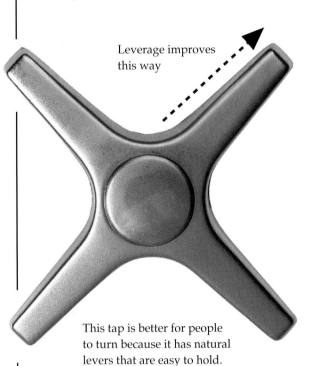

This tap is better for people to turn because it has natural levers that are easy to hold.

Easier turning

As people get older their hand muscles become weaker and they cannot grip so well. Here is a gadget that can be used to get a better grip on many things. Inside the case is a sponge. The steel pins rest on the sponge and when the case is pressed on a tap top, for example, some of the pins push on to the tap. This awkward tap shape can now be gripped by the turning gadget.

This is the centre of gravity (balancing point) of a traditional design of kettle.

This is the centre of gravity (balancing point) of a jug kettle.

Better balance

Traditional kettles now look old-fashioned to many people. Some modern kettles are designed to look more like jugs.

Get a traditional kettle and a jug kettle and find out which is easier for an old person to use.

Fill each kettle and then lift it. Try to decide which muscles you are using and how easy it is to keep the kettle balanced so that water does not spill from it. Old people have weak wrists and they are best at pulling objects straight up. Which kettle is more appropriate for them?

(For more information on measuring centres of gravity see the book Measuring in the Science in our world series*).*

Materials

Design involves using the right materials for each purpose. Every material has its own range of properties and these have to be understood in advance if the design is to produce a long lasting, safe and easy-to-use product.

(For more information about materials see the book Materials *in the Science in our world series).*

Beyond the needs of science

Some materials are good **electrical conductors** and others good **insulators**. In a **household circuit** both properties are needed. The casing for the wires and plug must be good insulators, but the plug pins, connectors and wires must be good conductors.

There are many designs of plugs and sockets in the world because the distance between the metal connectors needs only to be small to prevent **short circuits** of electricity. As a result there is much scope to provide varied designs.

This picture shows some design features of a plug and socket. The plug shape gives a good grip and it is large enough to make it easy to handle.

A range of designs

These three garlic presses are all designed to do the same job: they must crush cloves of garlic to be used in cooking.

To do this they use the principle of levers. The garlic is placed near the pivot of the device and the levers used to crush the garlic by gripping them as far from the hinge as possible. When different materials are used to make a tool, a different design is needed. Plastic, for example, must be thicker than steel when large forces are going to be applied or it will snap.

Look for design differences

Investigate a range of kitchen articles (such as serving spoons and knives) and see how many varieties you can find. Then examine the materials they are made of and see if you can discover how the designer has had to adapt the design to match the material.

Plastic spatula to prevent scratching pans.

A kitchen utensil made up of a range of materials. The properties of each material has influenced the design.

Plastic handle to prevent heat conduction and burning.

Metal shank for strength.

Plastic is light weight.

How to use models

Although it is possible to make trial designs using ladders and boards (as on page 14), for more complicated tasks it is better to make scale models. This will help solve many problems in the early stages of design.

An ergonome is a scale model of a person with joints that allow you to find out about reach and to decide on the size of a design.

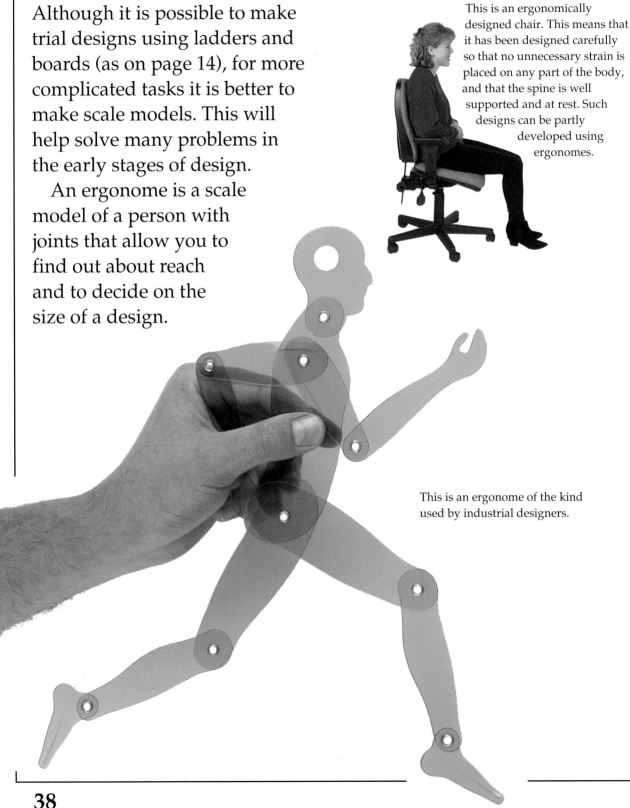

This is an ergonomically designed chair. This means that it has been designed carefully so that no unnecessary strain is placed on any part of the body, and that the spine is well supported and at rest. Such designs can be partly developed using ergonomes.

This is an ergonome of the kind used by industrial designers.

Design for a hall chair

Chairs in public buildings such as halls need to suit many types of audience. It is not possible to know the size of person that will sit in any of the chairs and so the design must be suitable for as many people as possible. Such chairs will be designed to suit 95% of all adults which is usually taken as the best **compromise** that can be made.

Measure the chairs in your hall or other public room and see if they match the design recommendation sizes shown below. If they do not match can you think why not?

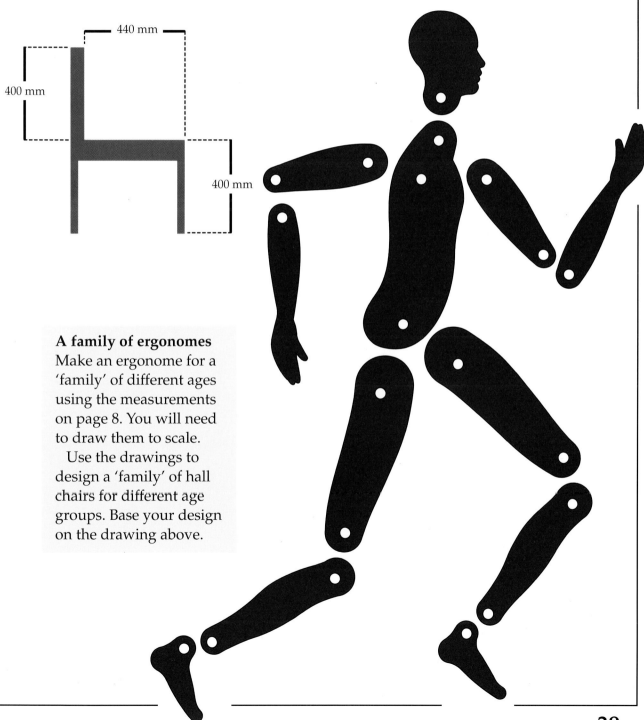

A family of ergonomes

Make an ergonome for a 'family' of different ages using the measurements on page 8. You will need to draw them to scale.

Use the drawings to design a 'family' of hall chairs for different age groups. Base your design on the drawing above.

Find out about work space

Many jobs that are done in a classroom, a kitchen or when people are at work require much moving from one place to another. It is therefore important to make sure everything is placed conveniently so that these jobs take as short a time and are as least tiring as possible.

One way this can be done is by finding out how much walking has to be done, and then, by using a model, try to plan a better arrangement for the room layout.

Using photography in discovery

The picture sequence shown below was taken to show the stages needed to make a cup of coffee. Photographing actions of complicated events can be a good way of recording information for later study.

Try photographing a friend while she or he is making a simple meal. Use a camera with a lens that covers a wide angle of view (an adult will help with this choice) and always stand in the same place. Use either regular print film or instant print.

Here the kettle is being filled. Why do you think the kettle should be taken so far from an electricity point. Is this good or bad design?

The kettle is plugged in and the coffee taken from the cupboard. Do you think the cupboard is too high or too low? Why doesn't the cupboard rest directly on the back of the work surface?

Cups are being fetched from the storage cupboard. Notice the dishwasher on the left of the sink. The dishwasher will be needed to wash the used cups.

This is the route that was taken to make a cup of coffee. Notice how little walking had to be done. This is a sign of good kitchen design.

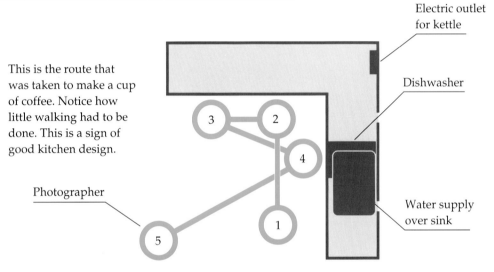

Electric outlet for kettle

Dishwasher

Water supply over sink

Photographer

The coffee is prepared and will now be taken to the table (which is where the photographer is standing, 5).

Designing a kitchen

Kitchens are one of the most used rooms of a house. The kitchen is the home's workshop, where many kinds of tools (appliances) and materials (food and crockery etc.) are stored.

In this environment it is important to make sure everything is safe and that the amount of effort needed to work is kept to a minimum. This will also help to prevent, for example, things like back strain and tired legs and feet. In fact all the problems you have seen about design come together in a kitchen. Can you now solve them?

Use this grid to work out the size of your kitchen. Each square has a side of half a metre. Kitchen units are made in standard sizes, as shown on the right.

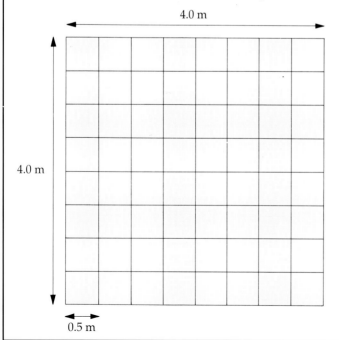

4.0 m

4.0 m

0.5 m

Easier preparation

Draw a scale plan of your kitchen by copying the 'room' shown below. Add the kitchen units and appliances in their correct places.

Stand in your kitchen and make yourself a hot drink. As you make the drink, notice where you walk and how many cupboards you have opened and closed. Mark on your scale plan the routes you have made. This route is a guide.

By looking at your route, do you think things are organised efficiently in your kitchen? Can you think of ways to place things so there is less moving about?

On your plan try to rearrange the kitchen units and appliances to make the distance walked as short as possible. Ask the adult who uses the kitchen most to explain how and why it was organised this way and discuss your new plan with them to see what they think.

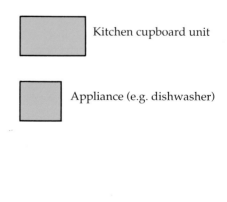

Kitchen cupboard unit

Appliance (e.g. dishwasher)

42

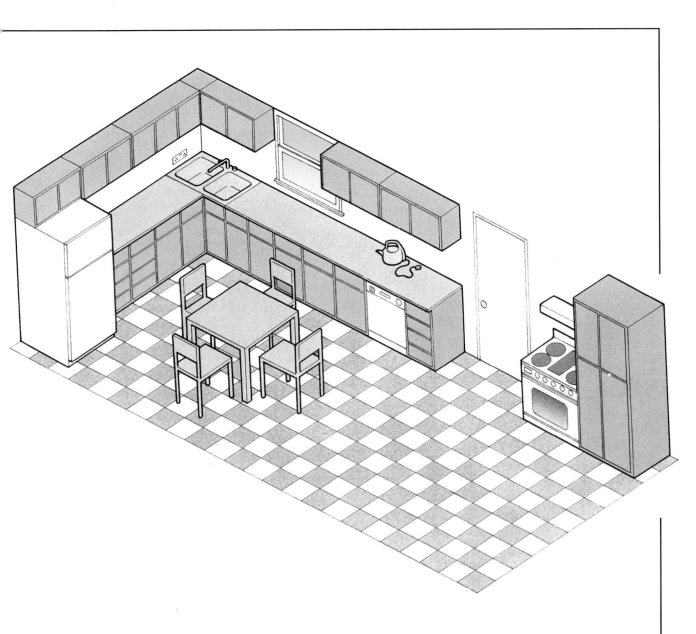

Redesign a kitchen

Trace this kitchen plan. First look carefully to see if you can see any safety problems with this kitchen. (For example, look carefully for electrical supplies too close to water, or where hot foods might be carried across the route taken by people walking through doors.)

Then, imagine you are making a simple meal of your choice . Draw the route that would be taken. Look at the route and then make a new tracing, this time redesigning the kitchen to make the journey as safe and as efficient as possible. (Use pages 40-41 as a guide.)

Garden design

Science and design are not only important in the home, the shops and places of work. They are equally important in the garden and the countryside. But here a different set of science rules apply.

This is how science can help at the planning stage of a garden. You need to think about the weather (sun, wind and rain), about how wild things grow together, and about how you want to use the garden.

A walled town garden.

Placing a pond
Natural ponds are usually much deeper and have a bigger area than garden ponds. This means that in the heat of a day the water in a garden pond may get too warm for fish and other wildlife. A pond placed in an open position may not be the best for the fish.

Locating a patio
A patio is a paved area where tables and chairs are placed. To get the most use of a patio it should be placed where the Sun reaches early in the morning. This makes it a pleasant place to have breakfast. But it needs to be shaded in the heat of the afternoon sun. A high hedge, a fence, a tree or the walls of the house can all be used for shade.

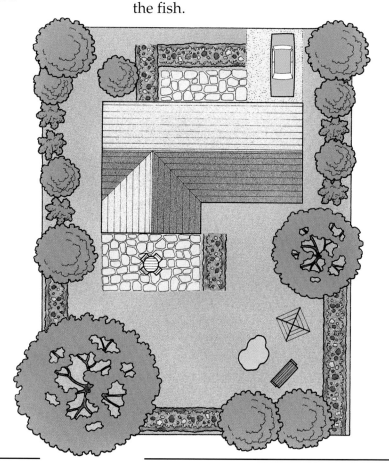

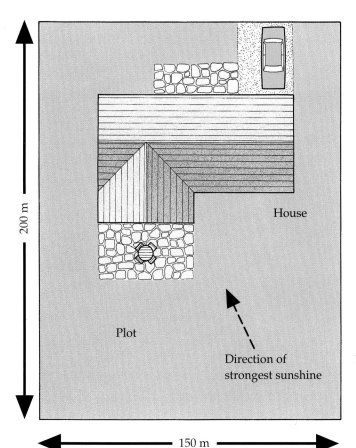

200 m

House

Plot

Direction of
strongest sunshine

150 m

Colourful flowers

Many colourful flowers are annuals, that
is they grow from seed each year. These
often thrive in hot sunny places well
away from shade, walls and hedges.

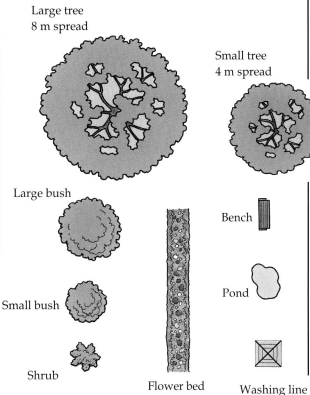

Large tree
8 m spread

Small tree
4 m spread

Large bush

Bench

Pond

Small bush

Shrub

Flower bed

Washing line

Group work

As a group draw a house plot on to a
large sheet of paper. Copy the landscape
shapes shown on this page and draw
them to the same scale as the plot.

Now agree where to place the patio,
the large shady tree, the pond, beds for
flowers that like sunshine and those that
will only grow in shade. Also make sure
the garden is suited to as many varieties
of birds as possible.

Evergreens

People use evergreen shrubs and trees
to give some colour to a garden all year
round, but most garden evergreens do not
provide a good source of food for birds.

Places for birds

It is fun watching birds in a garden, but it is important to provide many
different types of plant if you want to get a wide variety of birds to visit.
Some birds look for insects under plants, others search in trees, some like
open ground and others like undergrowth. In fact birds thrive the more
variety you can provide such as lawn, flower beds, shrubs and trees.

45

New words

average
the word average means the result of adding up the values of a group of objects and then dividing by the number of objects in the group. This is called the mean value by mathematicians

behaviour
the way people act. Behaviour normally refers to the normal day-to-day activities of people, but sometimes design has to take into account the behaviour of people in emergency situations such as a fire

centre of gravity
it is often useful to try to work out the place where the weight of an object acts. The term centre of gravity is used to describe this place. If the object has most of its weight high up, it is probably 'top heavy', that is it has its centre of gravity high up. If the weight is mostly low down, it is 'bottom heavy' with a centre of gravity low down. This position makes an object much less likely to fall over (gravity is the force produced by every object in the Universe. For objects on Earth the dominant force of gravity is towards the centre of the planet)

compress
to make smaller by applying a force. Most frequently a force is applied in just one direction so that compression results in squashing in the direction of the force but often this is balanced by expansion as, for example, dough is rolled out by a pastry roller

compromise
to take a view about something which is perhaps slightly less than ideal from any one point of view, but which, on balance, gets closest to meeting all the competing points of view

counterbalance
if an object is balanced it will have the same weight on both sides of the pivoting point. A counterbalance is a weight that is added to something to get it into balance. Counterbalances are used in many places. They can be found as a weight on the end of a bar, or a weight on the end of a cable running over a pulley

electrical conductor
a substance that allows electricity to flow freely through it. Metals are the most common conductors of electricity, although other substances, especially water, can also readily act as conductors. This is the reason it is dangerous to have kitchen plugs and switches near to places where water may be splashed or spilled or where the plugs and switches may be touched with wet hands

force
to make an object move some effort, or force, such as pulling or pushing has to be applied

household circuit

the household circuit is the main electricity supply in the home. It consists of an alternating current. Each country has its own standards for household supply voltage. The most common voltages used are 240 V and 110 V

insulator

a substance that does not conduct electricity very well. Most rocks, plastics and plant materials such as wood are good insulators. The air is also a good insulator which is why bare electrical supply cables can be hung from pylons

lever

this is a long bar which is used to enable people to move a heavy object more easily. The lever is used with a pivot. The lever is placed under the heavy object and over the pivot. The object is lifted by pressing down on the other end of the lever

mass

the amount of a substance. Mass is not the same as volume. The term mass is not commonly used because the effect of gravity acts on all substances on Earth and gives them a weight. In regions of space distant from stars and planets there is very little gravity and substances are then 'weightless' even though they keep the same mass

pivot

the place about which an object can rotate. An axle is a common pivot, but anything can act as a pivot. For example, the joints in your body are all pivots, as are the ends of chairs when they are rocked to and fro

range

the value that is obtained when you take the difference between the biggest value and the smallest value of a group of measurements

reach

the distance that a person can comfortably stretch out and do useful work. Usually reach is less than the furthest part that can be touched because no useful work can be done when fully stretched

short circuit

an accidental flow of electricity along an unintentional path

symmetrical

to be evenly shaped about a point or a line. Our bodies are roughly symmetrical about a line drawn from our heads through the centre of our bodies. A ball is symmetrical about any line that goes through its centre

weight

gravity acts on the substance of an object (its mass) to give it weight. A golf ball and a lump of lead of the same size will weigh different amounts because each has a different mass

Index